A brief look at

SOUTHDOWN

1975 to 1990

SOUTHDOWN LOCAL SERIES   Volume One

by Paul Llewellyn

PAUL LLEWELLYN PUBLISHING

Design by: JAC design, Crowborough

Printed in England by: Bishops Printers Ltd., Portsmouth

Introduction

Welcome to this first book entitled 'A Brief Look at Southdown' 1975 to 1990 Photograph Album.

Many books have been written about Southdown Motor Services Limited, but not many portray a collection of photographs taken by one person between 1975 to 1990!

I started my interest in Southdown in the early 1970's (when I was a teenager!), when every Saturday I would travel on a Leyland or Bristol Saloon from my home in High Hurstwood to Uckfield bus station on service 120 from Crowborough. Over a period of time, I got to know the Crowborough drivers well and with my little 126 Kodak instamatic took some photographs of some of the vehicles I travelled on. Some of these photos are in this book, and not very good quality, but they are a record of my interest in Southdown, which I wanted to share with you, the reader. As time went by, I travelled further afield by bus to explore Southdown's routes and vehicles and my photography did get better with the help of a 35mm Camera! Working on this book brought back some very happy memories of my trips out by bus as an enthusiast and as a driver working for Southdown in the East & Mid Sussex Division – good company and employer – until August 1989 when Southdown was sold to the Stagecoach Group.

Book one illustrates the last of SMS colours to standard NBC green and back to SMS colours after deregulation in 1985. Book two will follow on from there!

I felt this book needed to be put together for future generations to enjoy, not just for bus enthusiasts, but for local historians as well.

My thanks go to Richard Maryan, Norman Stanbridge, Scott McAvoy and Peter Dann, for the use of their photographs.

Also to Tom Dann, who helped with the computer work in putting this book together and understanding how I wanted the book to look!

Paul Llewellyn

Crowborough
East Sussex
January 2010

199 KUF 199F – 1968 Leyland Leopard. In 1985 Southdown celebrated its 70th anniversary by holding a special event on June 2nd 1985 at Brighton seafront. Although this vehicle was on the disposal list at the time, the Company allowed a few members of staff at Horsham depot to repaint the vehicle to appear at this special event. The bus was then sold to members of staff for preservation.

484 TCD 484J – 1970 Bristol RESL6L arriving at Chichester Bus Station after operating a service from Bosham, on 16th November 1985.

486 TCD 486J – Operating the last conventional bus on service 149 Uckfield to Uckfield via High Hurstwood and Fairwarp before the new East Sussex County Council County Rider service network started. Photograph taken at Fairwarp Crossroads on 24th November 1984.

492 UCD 602J – 1971 Bristol RELL6L with ECW bodywork on service 309 from Havant to Waterlooville on 30th September 1985 in Havant.

0439 NUF 439G – Bristol RELL6G with Marshall bodywork was converted to the Uckfield staff restroom in the 1980s.

30 PCD 76R – 1976 Leyland National on service 121 to Lewes. Photograph taken at the King's Head at Chailey on 5th October 1985. In Unibus advert for "Langney Shopping Centre".

36 PCD 82R – 36 was allocated to the Haywards Heath depot and on Sundays the depot worked various tendered contracts for Kent County Council during the late 1980s. This photo was taken in Rusthall, Tunbridge Wells on the 10th of April, 1988.

43 RUF 43R – 1977 Leyland National with centre doors on a Haywards Heath to Pease Pottage service on 8th October 1985. 43, when new, was allocated to Brighton and then spent the latter years at Haywards Heath.

64 WYJ 164S – 1978 Leyland National with centre doors about to enter Chichester bus station after completing a local service 248 in April 1985.

84 YCD 84T – On service 189 between Haywards Heath and Horsham. 84 was photographed at Prongers Corner near Horsham on 15th of April 1985.

93 AYJ 93T – At Slindon Common near Chichester on 12th April 1988.

123 HFG 923V – Southdown had a small number of Leyland National Mk 2s. This one was noted on service 744 from Wecock Farm, Waterlooville to Portsmouth 30th September 1985.

126 JWV 126W – This is the author's favourite vehicle in the Southdown fleet, a Mk 2 Leyland National on a County Rider service 249 Uckfield to Uckfield via the villages of High Hurstwood and Fairwarp. This photograph was taken at Fairwarp Crossroads on 28th May 1987.

143 GKE 501L – This vehicle was new to Maidstone & District in 1973 and was acquired by Southdown in 1981. 143 is operating service 190 from Uckfield to Eastbourne at Vine's Corner, Heathfield on 12th October 1985.

911 C591 SHC – 1986 Mercedes Benz L608D allocated to Haywards Heath and would normally operate the local services in Haywards Heath. 911 was noted operating service 33 Willow Way in Hurstpierpoint on 28th May 1988.

802 B802 GFG – Southdown operated a number of County Rider vehicles for East Sussex County Council on contract services. 802 was loaned to Maidstone & District at Tunbridge Wells to operate service 290 from Tunbridge Wells to Groombridge after the closure of the railway line between Eridge, Groombridge and Tunbridge Wells in 1985. This photograph was taken at Groombridge station on 31st July 1985.

0830 (NYV 459) Bedford SHZ towing 3113 NUF 452G a Leyland Leopard, back to Eastbourne from Chillies Farm, High Hurstwood in April 1981, after being involved in an accident.

T880 2880 CD – Leyland PD3/4 used as a driver training vehicle and Passenger Survey Bus at Chichester, May 1985.

0813 UF 4813 – 1929 Leyland Titan TD1 Company preserved vehicle on a private hire at Turner's Hill, West Sussex on August 10th, 1986.

1201 OLL 479L – Acquired from National Travel London in 1979, this Leyland Leopard PSU5/4R is arriving at Chichester bus station while working a local school service in April 1985.

1256 CUF 256L – A 1973 Leyland Leopard PSU3B/4R with Duple Dominant bodywork in Southdown Universal Livery working a relief National Express service from London to Eastbourne via Uckfield crossing the old Uckfield level crossing on 12th October 1985.

1361 TFG 221X – 1982 Leyland Leopard with Plaxton Supreme V bodywork seen here on a private hire at the old Tunbridge Wells West station on 27th June 1985.

1009 419 DCD – 1984 Leyland Tiger with Duple Laser bodywork. The original registration number was A809 CCD, which was reregistered with a PD3 number plate 419 DCD in 1987. 1009 was photographed at Southsea on 2nd June 1990 and had just worked on service 075 from London Victoria.

3201 401 DCD – 1964 Leyland Titan PD3/4 on a private hire to the village of Fletching on 6th July 1985.

112 112 CUF – 1964 Leyland Leopard with Marshall bodywork. These Leopards were a regular feature on Southdown country routes during the 1960s and 70s. 112 is seen parked up in Bell Lane, Uckfield on a Sunday morning in July 1975. (Bell Lane is now the link road between the town centre and the Uckfield bypass, how times have changed!).

144 EUF 144D – 1965 Leyland Leopard with Weymann bodywork. 144 was involved in a serious accident in 1967 and was re-bodied with a Marshall body as seen here in Luxford Road, Crowborough, in May 1976.

180 KCD 180F – 180 on service 149 Crowborough – High Hurstwood – Uckfield – Lewes and is photographed at Chillies Farm, High Hurstwood in June 1979. This group of services 119/129/139/149 were the last group of services which Crowborough depot operated until the closure of the depot in May 1980.

188 KCD 188F – 188 is seen on the Crowborough local service 151 on its layover in Fermor Road, Crowborough in March 1975.

190 KCD 190F – At Petersfield Station on service 59 to Brighton in the early 1970s. (Photo courtesy of Norman Stanbridge).

195 KUF 195F – 1968 Leyland Leopard with Willowbrook bodywork. Leopards were regular sights on Southdown operated B.A.T.S routes in the Brighton area. 195 Is about to depart Pool Valley for West Dene in March 1976.

206 KUF 206F – During May/June of each year Southdown would relicense some of the older vehicles on the disposal list for covering vehicles attending the Derby. 206 had been in store at Hayling Island and was one such vehicle to "reappear" for a two month period. 206 is working a service 288 shopper bus to Chichester and is seen at Wisborough Green in West Sussex in June 1980. (Photo courtesy of Norman Stanbridge).

221 KUF 221F – 1968 Bristol RESL6G with Marshall bodywork. 221 is parked up in Bell Lane, Uckfield in April 1976.

224 KUF 224F – 1968 Bristol RESL with Marshall bodywork photographed at Horsham Carfax in January 1977.

458 NUF 458G – 458 is operating service 120 (Tuesdays, Thursdays and Saturdays) to Uckfield via High Hurstwood from Crowborough. Photo taken at the Maypole pub, High Hurstwood on 21st April 1973. (Photo courtesy of Richard Maryan).

463 PUF 163H – 1969 Leyland Leopard with Northern Counties bodywork. Photographed at Hassocks station forecourt in March 1976.

3118 PUF 171H – This vehicle was originally numbered 471 and was renumbered to 3118 during 1979 as an FDV (Fully Depreciated Vehicle) and was used on school work and seasonal services. A number of vehicles were used in this way. Service 220 was a summer service in the Chichester area and the photo was taken at Goodwood racecourse in the summer of 1981.

2204 PPM 204G – Photographed in Bognor Regis bus station in the summer of 1979.

2208 PPM 208G – Seen here at High Hurstwood Post Office on service 150 to Crowborough in 1975. 2208 was used for nearly a year on the Crowborough local service 151 until it joined its "sisters" in the Portsmouth area.

488 TCD 488J – Seen at Brighton Pool Valley working service 38 to Bevendean Hospital in 1978.

491 UCD 601J – 1971 Bristol RELL6L with ECW bodywork. These vehicles were used in the Brighton area when new and then transferred to country depots towards the end of their working lives with Southdown. 491 is seen on service 12A at Woodingdean, Brighton in July 1984.

2212 TCD 612J – Bristol RESL with ECW bodywork seen here in Brighton Pool Valley on service 38 to Bevendean Hospital in the autumn of 1977.

12 BCD 812L – Number 12 is operating service 222 "the Downsman" that operated and linked up various attractions and villages in West Sussex in the early 1980s. This view was taken at Upwaltham near Chichester in the spring of 1985. (Photo courtesy of Norman Stanbridge).

16 BCD 816L – 1973 Leyland National. This view of National 16 is at High Salvington whilst working service 206 from Worthing in July 1984.

17 BCD 817L – The first batch of Leyland Nationals delivered to Southdown came in the "drab" all over National bus green as shown in this picture. 17 has just arrived from Worthing on service 212 to Arundel. Photograph was taken in Jarvis Road, Arundel in September 1983.

161 MOD 822P – Photographed at Mark Cross on 18th April 1987 whilst operating service 227 Mark Cross – Rotherfield – Crowborough. 161 was new to Western National Omnibus Ltd and was acquired by Southdown in October 1986.

29 PCD 75R – Looking rather smart in its traditional Southdown green and cream livery, National 29 is about to depart on service 615 from Rusthall to Willow Lea in Tonbridge on Sunday 10th April 1988.

31 PCD 77R – National 31 (Ex Langley Shopping Unibus advert) had just received its repaint into SMS colours and was operating service 19A Uckfield to Crowborough in July 1987.

78 YCD 78T – After just completing the St. Pauls school contract, 78 was running "light" to Crowborough to operate on the local service. The photograph was taken on the Ashdown Forest at Fairwarp in May 1987.

82 YCD 82T – 82 is parked up at Henfield depot on Sunday 14th February 1988.

114 ENJ 914V – On service 266 East Grinstead to Uckfield at Red Lion, Chelwood Gate in September 1987.

651 LWV 651P – 1976 Ford A 0609 Alexander minibus. 650 and 651 had a very short life with Southdown and were sold to Western National during 1977. This photo of 651 is at the Portslade Works open day on Saturday 4th September 1976.

1218 EUF 218D – 1966 Leyland Leopard PSU3/3R with Plaxton Panorama bodywork at Worthing depot, having just arrived from Chichester on a private hire in May 1974.

3004 LCD 242F – 1968 Leyland Leopard with Plaxton Panorama bodywork. Originally numbered 1242 and was renumbered to 3004 during 1978 as an FDV (Fully Depreciated Vehicle) and could be found working on school work and works contracts in the Portsmouth area. 3004 was just arriving back from such a duty at Emsworth Depot in May 1979.

1839 UUF 339J – 1971 Leyland Leopard with Panorama Elite bodywork. 1839 is seen at Conway Street in 1983.

1282 RYJ 882R – 1977 Leyland Leopard with Duple Dominant bodywork. The National Bus Company decided that Southdown should have some Grant Coaches for rural services. This batch of vehicles was the first to be delivered to Southdown during the latter part of 1977. 1282 is outside Portslade works waiting to receive transfers for service "Stagecoach 799."

1304 ANJ 304T & 1263 CUF 263L. After passing My PSV in June 1986 I worked at Lewes depot and did school contracts from various primary schools in the Brighton area to various sports facilities in the Brighton town. On this particular day we visited Brighton Wild Park on the Lewes Road. Whilst taking the photograph, the schoolchildren were doing their sporting activities. Photograph was taken in July 1986.

1316 ANJ 316T – Service 849 was normally operated by a Leyland Redline Cub (County Rider). On this day, the vehicle was not available, so a Grant Coach sporting the East and Mid Sussex colours was used instead. Photograph taken on March 11th, 1986.

1300 YYJ 300T – 1978 Leyland Leopard with Plaxton Supreme bodywork. 1300 on a Sussex Link private hire to Birling Gap near Eastbourne on the 5th of March 1988. Southdown coach livery after deregulation was a boring plain white with a few green stripes and the lettering "Southdown Coaches" on it until the lovely two-tone dark green was used later on.

0421 421 DCD Tree Lopper – Working at Hellingly Hospital area near Hailsham, pruning back the trees so that double deckers could operate on this route. Trees normally have to be pruned back over the winter months. This photograph was taken during February 1988.

3209 409 DCD & 3215 415 DCD – At Chichester depot on 5th July 1986. 3209 was working on a private hire from Uckfield, and the opportunity arose to have a photograph taken with "sister" vehicle 3215 in a similar livery sporting a "Beautiful Britain" advert.

2003 OPN 803 – 1959 Bristol LDS6B with ECW bodywork being used on service 17 to King Alfred Lagoon during summer 1976.

2051 AAP 51B – 1963 Bristol FS6B with ECW bodywork de-licensed in Moulsecoomb depot in 1977.

548 LFS 300F – 1968 Bristol VRT with ECW bodywork, acquired from Eastern Scottish Bus Company in 1973, on service 100 that operated between Brighton and Steyning. 548 was photographed in Pool Valley in 1976.

522 WCD 522K – 522 is a 1971 Bristol VRT, photographed at Conway Street, Hove, in May 1984.

541 WUF 541K – 541 is a 1972 Bristol VRT with centre doors, de-licensed at Hayling Island, Hampshire on 17th March 1985.

569 GNJ 569N – 1974 Bristol VRT in Portsmouth area Travel card livery at Hambledon in Hampshire on 2nd September 1985.

583 GNJ 583N – 1975 Bristol VRT SL3/510 turbo charged in Brolac Paints advert livery at Portslade in 1984.

617 UWV 617S – Open-top Bristol VRT working service 209 Worthing summer months service on 1st September 1985.

634 XAP 634S – A number of these VRs were painted up in National Holidays livery. 634 is one of the examples photographed at Hambledon depot in Hampshire in the autumn of 1984.

683 EAP 983V – 683 at Selsey Bill near Chichester on service 250. 683 is advertising the local daily newspaper "The Evening Argus" in May 1983.

260 JWV 260W – 260 showing its Mile Oak Shuttle livery which was supported by East Sussex County Council in the early 1980s. This view shows it parked up near Conway Street in May 1984.

274 JWV 274W – 1981 Bristol VRT SL3/680 with ECW bodywork. These were the last Bristol VRs to be delivered to Southdown. 274 has vinyl posters advertising Stagecoach 700 coastliner. Photograph was taken in Pool Valley in May 1984.

730 SCD 730N – In 1975 a new limited stop service 700 operated between Brighton and Portsmouth. Southdown introduced their new Leyland Atlanteans to this route and marketed it as Coastliner 700. 730 waits in Pool Valley for its departure to Portsmouth in February 1976.

734 SCD 734N – Steyning was a small outstation where normally two Atlanteans were based to operate service 100 to Brighton. 734 was photographed at the outstation in May 1982 and as you can see there are works going on the background as this was the start of the work for the Steyning bypass. The outstation no longer exists.

743 LCD 43P – This was the last batch of Atlanteans delivered to Southdown and 743 departs from Hilsea heading towards Westbourne on service 357, although the vehicle is advertising X71 service Solenteer Portsmouth to Southampton service. Photograph was taken in May 1979.

746 LCD 46P – 746 operating service 744 to Portsmouth, photographed at Waterlooville on 2nd September 1985.

3204 404 DCD – Working a railway replacement service from Falmer station to Brighton station in 1985.

3206 WRU 702B – Originally 406 DCD, the number plate was transferred to a coach. 3206 is working the open top service Eastbourne Pier to Birling Gap via Beachy Head during the summer of 1986.

3209 409 DCD – Received "Maritime England" promotional livery for the Cinque Ports along the South Coast. 409 was photographed at Sheffield Park Bus Rally (Bluebell Railway) on 13th May 1984.

3215 415 DCD – Painted up in the "Beautiful Britain" campaign, seen here leaving the 70th anniversary event at Brighton Seafront on June 2nd 1985.

3217 417 DCD – Seen here leaving the 70th anniversary event at Brighton Seafront on June 2nd 1985.

3226 RPN 10 – 3226 working service 77 from Devil's Dyke to Rottingdean on 29th September 1985.

3227 RPN 11 – 1960 Bristol Lodekka FS6G with ECW bodywork. Part of the Company's 70th anniversary, they reintroduced route 24 Brighton to Brighton via Lewes and the surrounding villages. This view is taken on Devil's Dyke Road on the last day of service, 29th September 1985.

3229 SPM 22 – Seen here leaving the 70th anniversary event at Brighton Seafront providing free bus rides around the area on June 2nd 1985.

539 WUF 539K – 1972 Bristol VR. This vehicle spent most of its working life in the Brighton area but did spend a period of time at Eastbourne and is shown here working service 190 from Uckfield to Eastbourne in 1985.

563 NCD 563M – Seen here at Conway Street on a winters day (10/2/85) bearing the Eagle Star Insurance Company advert.

581 GNJ 581N – 1975 Bristol VR with 510 turbo charged engine. In Patcham on 28th December 1985 on service 5B.

586 PUF 586R – 1977 Bristol VR displaying Unibus Advert for Uncle Sam's Burgers at Brighton Old Steine in 1984.

607 UWV 607S – Southdown had a very big presence with coaches and open-top vehicles at the annual Derby races on the first Wednesday of June. This photograph was taken on the 5th June 1985. (Since then, the Derby has been transferred to the first Saturday of June.)

616 UWV 616S – 1978 Bristol VR convertible open-top in open-top form on service 77 at Devils Dyke in the summer of 1983.

621 UWV 621S – 1978 Bristol VR convertible open-top in open-top form. Just arriving at Brighton 70th Anniversary event on June 2nd 1985 sporting the "1066 promotional advert livery."

623 UWV 623S – 1978 Bristol VR convertible open-top in closed-top form. Seen here at Newick Green on service 169 Haywards Heath to Uckfield service on 1st October 1985.

626 UFG 626S – 1977 Bristol VR with centre doors, working service 25 arriving at Falmer station on 13th April 1985.

660 AAP 660T – 1978 Bristol VR sporting Radio Victory advert livery passing through the village of Denmead near Hambledon in Hampshire on 30th September 1985.

663 AAP 663T – 1979 Bristol VR sporting TSB Trust card advert livery on service 5B at Patcham in 1985.

685 EAP 985V – 1980 Bristol VR sporting unfinished Portsmouth Area Travel card awaiting transfers. Seen here at Wecock Farm, Waterlooville in September 1985.

256 JWV 256W – 1980 Bristol VR sporting vinyl's for Stagecoach 700 Coastliner and Southdown West Sussex fleet names at Worthing sea front on 28th December 1985.

716 PUF 716M – 1974 Leyland Atlantean with Park Royal bodywork seen here at Wecock Farm in Waterlooville on 30th September 1985.

706 PUF 136M – Parked up at Hayling Island depot in June 1983.

738 SUF 138N – On service 12 bound for Southwick Square at the Old Steine in Brighton on 28th December 1985.

745 LCD 45P – 1975 Leyland Atlantean with Park Royal-Roe bodywork, these were the last Atlanteans that were delivered to Southdown. On service 744 at Wecock Farm, Waterlooville on 30th September 1985.

Southdown House – Freshfield Road, Brighton. This was Southdown's head office, photograph taken on 28th December, 1985. The building has since been demolished.

This view shows, the 'Author', in his younger days in the winter of 1986/87. Having just arrived at work to take out National 117 (ENJ 917V) on Service 19 to Eastbourne. The crew room at Uckfield was a 1969 Bristol RE – 0439 – NUF 439G and it was sold for scrap in May 1987. Photo courtesy of Peter Dann.